# The Magnificat

MY SOUL MAGNIFIES THE LORD,

AND MY SPIRIT REJOICES IN GOD MY SAVIOR,

FOR HE HAS LOOKED WITH FAVOR ON THE LOWLINESS OF HIS SERVANT.

FROM NOW ON, ALL GENERATIONS WILL CALL ME BLESSED;

FOR THE MIGHTY ONE HAS DONE GREAT THINGS FOR ME

AND HOLY IS HIS NAME.

Sources for the life and times of Mary are taken from the four gospels, the Apocryphal New Testament

(in particular the Protevangelium of James), and the Golden Legend by Jacobus de Voragine.

# MARY

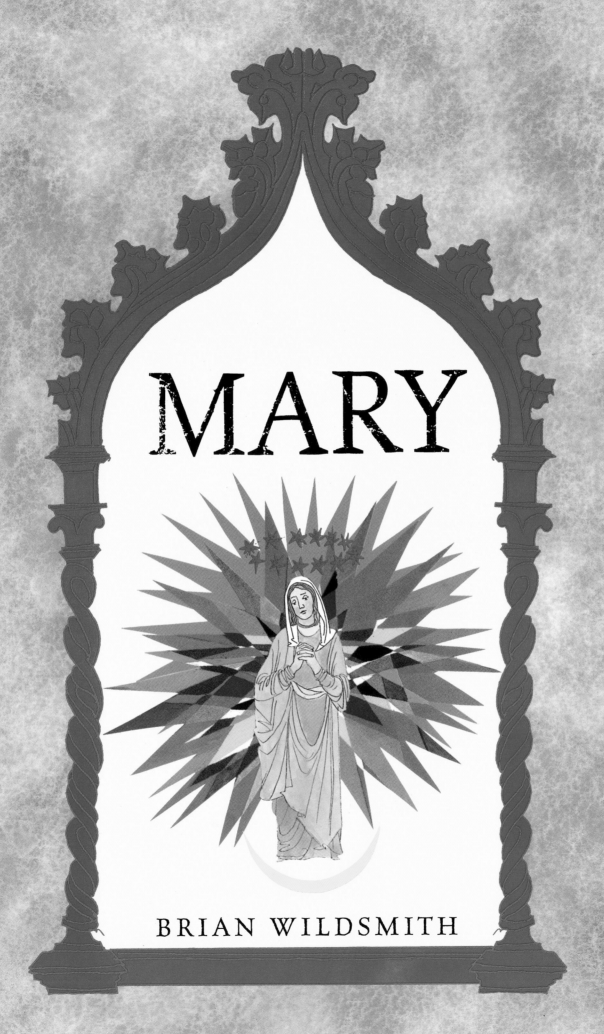

## BRIAN WILDSMITH

**EERDMANS BOOKS FOR YOUNG READERS**
GRAND RAPIDS, MICHIGAN / CAMBRIDGE, U. K.

Once, a long time ago, a woman named Anna and her husband, Joachim, lived in Jerusalem. They were happy together, but they had no children.

One day Anna saw a nest of baby sparrows in her garden. She wept and wished that she too could have a baby. As she was wiping away her tears, an angel appeared and said to her, "Anna, the Lord has heard your prayers. You will have a daughter, and her name shall be known in all the world."

That same day Joachim was in the desert, looking after his flock. An angel came to him too and told him that Anna was going to have a baby.

Joachim hurried back to Jerusalem and saw Anna standing at the Golden Gate. They ran to each other, happy that they would have a child at last.

Anna gave birth to a baby girl and called her Mary. When the little girl was six months old she took her first steps.

When Mary was three, her parents took her to the temple. The priest placed her on the third step of the altar, and the little girl began to dance.

The years passed, and Mary grew up to be a beautiful young woman. A man named Joseph, who lived in Nazareth, loved her very much. They were betrothed to marry each other.

One moonlit night the angel Gabriel appeared before Mary and said, "Hail Mary, full of grace, the Lord has chosen you. You will have a son, and you will name him Jesus. He will be the Son of God."

Then Mary said, "Here am I, the servant of the Lord."

The next day Mary ran to see her cousin Elizabeth, who was also having a baby. They shared their joy and were happy for each other.

When it was almost time for Mary's baby to be born, Mary and Joseph had to make a long journey to Bethlehem to register for a census. When they arrived there was no room for them at the inn, so they had to sleep in a stable.

In the nearby hills that night, while shepherds were guarding their sheep, angels appeared in the sky to tell them that the Son of God had been born in Bethlehem. The shepherds hurried to the town and found the baby Jesus lying in a manger, with Mary and Joseph at his side.

Meanwhile, three wise men from the east saw a special star and traveled to Jerusalem to find the newborn king. They asked King Herod where the child could be. Herod told them to go to Bethlehem and come back and tell him if they found him. The wise men left and followed the shining star which led them to Jesus. They knelt before him and offered him gifts of gold, frankincense, and myrrh.

When Jesus was eight days old, Mary and Joseph took him to the temple and dedicated him to God by offering two turtledoves.

Later, an angel spoke to Joseph in a dream and warned him that Herod's soldiers had orders to kill Jesus. The angel told Joseph to take his family to Egypt, where Jesus could be safe.

Far away in Egypt, Mary cared for Jesus and sang songs to comfort him.

When Jesus was a little boy, the angel spoke to Joseph again and told him it was safe for his family to return to Nazareth because Herod was dead.

At home in Nazareth, Mary looked after the family. She wove cloth and sewed it to make their clothes. She drew water from the well, and she cooked their meals. Mary also made sure that Jesus learned to read and write.

Jesus was a kind and generous boy. He helped Joseph in his workshop, and Mary baked cakes for them.

When Jesus was twelve, his parents took him to Jerusalem for the Passover festival. When it was finished, Mary and Joseph began the trip home, not realizing that Jesus had stayed behind. They went back and found Jesus in the temple asking the teachers hard questions.

As Jesus grew up, he realized that he had to leave home and go out and preach the gospel of God's love. Mary was sad to see him go but knew that this was the right thing for him to do.

But Jesus never forgot about Mary, his mother. When he was invited to a wedding at Cana, he asked her to go with him. When the wine ran out, Mary was the first to notice and told Jesus. "Fill these jars with water," said Jesus. And the water turned to wine.

Jesus continued traveling, spreading God's message of love. Then one day he heard that Joseph was dying. He hurried back home to comfort his mother.

Jesus always remembered Joseph. Once, as Jesus was speaking to a large crowd, he told them how much Joseph had loved his family. "This is how you must live," he said. Mary was very moved when she heard this.

As time went by, the chief priests in Jerusalem started to plot against Jesus. They thought he was a threat to them, and they decided to have him killed. Mary came down to Jerusalem, but it was too late. Jesus had been arrested already and was carrying his cross through the streets. Mary watched as a goldfinch plucked out one of the thorns that pierced his head.

The sky grew dark and the earth trembled as Jesus was crucified. Before he died Jesus asked John, his beloved disciple, to promise to look after Mary.

When they took Jesus down from the cross, Mary held the dead body of her son in her arms and wept.

They placed Jesus's body in a tomb, but on the third day he rose from the dead. He appeared to Mary and his friends and then later went up to heaven.

At the feast of Pentecost, Mary and the disciples were all together. Suddenly there was a sound like a great wind. Tongues of fire flashed, and the Holy Spirit entered them all.

The apostles loved Mary and looked after her as she grew older. When the time came for her to die, they all gathered round to say goodbye. Mary passed away peacefully, knowing that she was soon to join her son.

Peter and John carried her to a tomb outside Jerusalem, and there they kept watch. A great choir of angels appeared in the sky, and Mary was taken up to heaven.

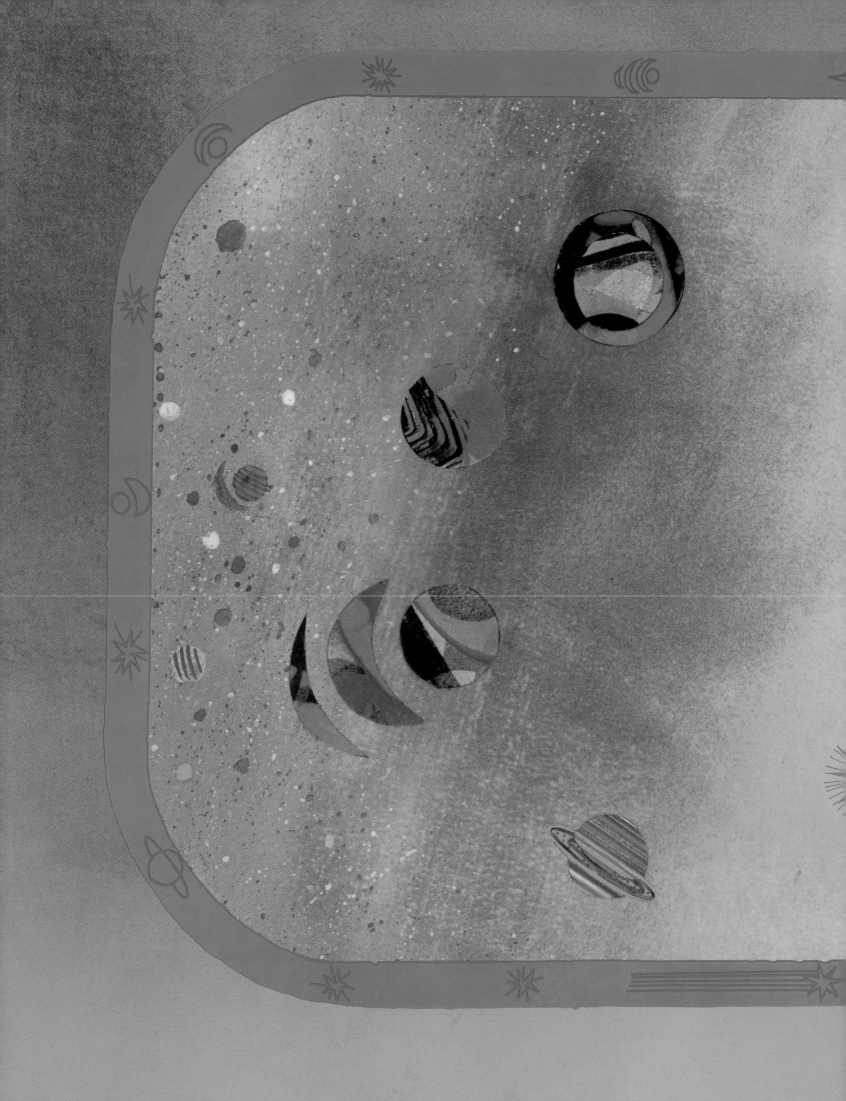

When she entered heaven, Mary was crowned Queen of Heaven and Earth, the eternal mother who watches over us all.

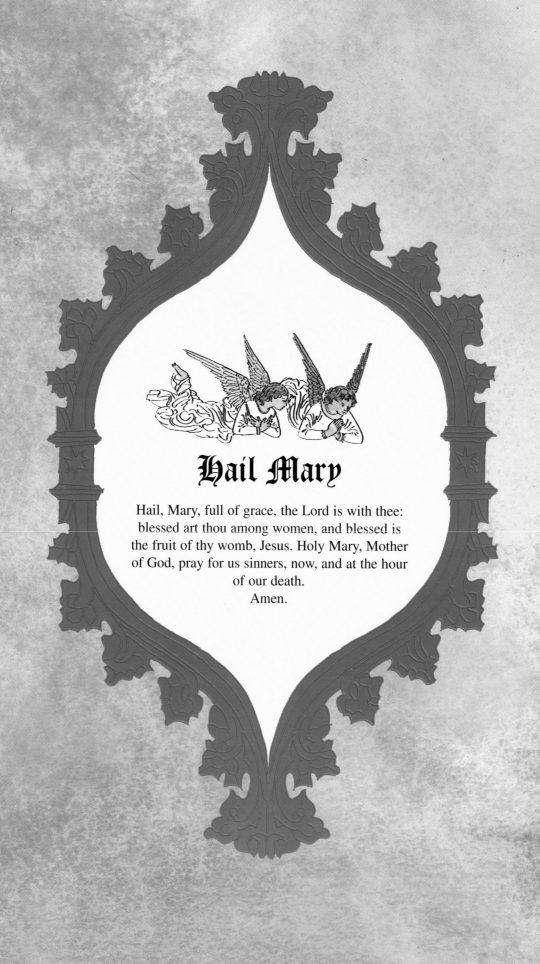

# Hail Mary

Hail, Mary, full of grace, the Lord is with thee:
blessed art thou among women, and blessed is
the fruit of thy womb, Jesus. Holy Mary, Mother
of God, pray for us sinners, now, and at the hour
of our death.
Amen.

© 2002 Brian Wildsmith

Published jointly in 2002
in the United Kingdom by
Oxford University Press
Great Claredon Street, Oxford OX2 6DP U.K.
and in the United States of America by
Eerdmans Books for Young Readers
An imprint of Wm. B. Eerdmans Publishing Co.
255 Jefferson Ave. S.E., Grand Rapids, Michigan 49503
P.O. Box 163, Cambridge CB3 9PU U.K.

02 03 04 05 06 07 08    7 6 5 4 3 2 1

A catalog record for this book is available
from the Library of Congress
ISBN 0-8028-5231-9